Navigating the
through central London

Rules, hazards, distances, and places
between Margaret Ness and Putney Bridge

ROBERT LUDLOW

Imray Laurie Norie & Wilson Ltd

Published by
Imray, Laurie, Norie & Wilson Ltd
Wych House, St Ives,
Cambridgeshire, PE27 5BT, England.
☎ +44 (0)1480 462114 Fax +44(0)1480 496109
Email ilnw@imray.com
www.imray.com
2012

ISBN 978 184623 489 7

British Library Cataloguing in Publication Data
A catalogue record for this book is available from the British Library.

For more information about rules and regulations on The Thames, skippers should be aware of current Notices to Mariners, The Port of London River Byelaws, General Directions for Navigation in the Port of London, and Port of London Authority Permanent Notice to mariners. There is also a useful and handy *River Thames Recreational Users Guide: Teddington to Sea Reach* (2011).

For those able to navigate under the bridges, the PLA's *Mariners' Guide to Bridges on the Tidal Thames* is recommended.

Local Charts, and all of these publications are available at or through the PLA website, www.pla.co.uk

The PLA's website aimed at leisure users, www.boatingonthethames.co.uk is another worthwhile source of information.

Photo on previous page – Greenwich

The Thames Barrier

Introduction

I have produced this small book principally as a help to leisure boaters who are not familiar with The Thames through central London. However, Part 2 may well help even the most seasoned of watermen.

The length of the river covered is from Margaret Ness in the east, to Putney Bridge in the west. This is the area for which a local knowledge endorsement is required for most commercial skippers. It is a very busy part of the Thames, with every conceivable type of craft likely to be encountered.

The book is divided into three parts. The first part gives general information and advice, and in passing, mentions local rules which will be relevant.

The second part lists many places the names of which you might read or hear on the radio, especially whilst monitoring 'London VTS' and Commercial Traffic on Ch 14, and helps quick location of that place on a chart. It is one thing to have the correct charts on board, but quite another to find the place mentioned quickly.

So for example if you hear of divers surveying Nelson Pier, with an associated request to keep wash to a minimum, with the assistance of this list, the position of Nelson Pier can be found rather more speedily than by simply pouring over your charts, wondering just where to start the search. As the idea is to help find places quickly, I have given the positions by reference to well-known landmarks, and in every case, have described them as up-stream from one such landmark, and downstream from another. In this way, I hope, it will be easy to pin-point the place in question whether you are proceeding up-, or downstream, yourself.

As additional aids, I have also given

a the longitude in minutes, and 1/10th of a minute, E or W for each entry.
   For all entries, the longitude is 0°.
   I HAVE NOT given the latitude

b the reach of the River

c the N or S bank, or, in the case of buoys/tiers/moorings, the N or S side of the river

d the approximate distance of the place from London Bridge. Positive values are for places downstream of London Bridge: negative are upstream. Using this data, one can quickly calculate the distance between 2 points, and so estimate journey-times. (eg From Delta Wharf (5·3) to Chelsea Harbour Pier (−4·7) is 10 nautical miles)

Distances are given in whole cables and so are NOT precise. For the purpose of this book, they need not be. The aim is to get you, the reader to the right area on your chart as quickly as possible, or to estimate (albeit to a reasonable accuracy), the length of your journey, nothing more.

The third part outlines the types of hazard you will encounter as you make your way up river. This IS NOT to be taken as an exhaustive or full list. It is indicative only. The fact that a hazard may be encountered which is not mentioned cannot be laid at my door. The rule must always be to keep a good watch at all times, both from your boat, and at Port of London Authority Notices to Mariners.

Please let me know of any amendments, or suggestions for improvement and additional places to be included.

My thanks go to my wife Jane, who has put up with me compiling this data, and to David Phillips, Chief Harbour Master of the PLA, who encouraged me, cast his eye over the work, and kindly described the book as 'a great contribution'.

Robert Ludlow, 2012
www.swanningabout.co.uk
info@swanningabout.co.uk

London Bridge

1 General advice

Sound Signals

These are the sound signals you are likely to hear, and indeed, should use in appropriate circumstances. They are principally those set out in the Collision Regulations, but with local additions.

•	I am altering my course to STARBOARD
• •	I am altering my course to PORT
• • •	I am operating ASTERN propulsion
• • • • •	I am turning fully round to STARBOARD
• • • • • •	I am turning fully round to PORT
• • • • •	I do not understand your intentions; keep clear; (I doubt whether you are taking sufficient action to avoid a collision)
▬	I am about to get underway/enter the fairway or I am approaching a blind bend
▬ • •	I am unable to manoeuvre (not under command)
▬ ▬ •	I intend to overtake you on your STARBOARD side
▬ ▬ • •	I intend to overtake you on your PORT side
▬ • ▬ •	I agree to be overtaken

The Thames Barrier *Patrick Roach*

St Georges Wharf, Nine Elms

Exclusion Zones

Except in case of emergency, or with the VTS's permission, do not enter any Exclusion Zones. Permanent Exclusion Zones are on the north of the river immediately upstream of Westminster Bridge, and immediately downstream of Vauxhall Bridge (south side). See your charts and Notices to Mariners.

Rowers

Blackwall, Greenwich, Battersea and Wandsworth reaches are used extensively by rowing clubs. The boats they use have very little freeboard, and are susceptible to wash from other craft. See note below about speed limits and wash.

When it all goes wrong!

- If you have engine or other mechanical failure, drop an anchor, and let 'London VTS' on Ch 14 know immediately. Follow their instructions. Do

not try to sort things out, whilst allowing your boat to drift with the tide. There is no surer way of allowing a hitch to develop into total disaster.

- If you have an accident, let 'London VTS' know on Ch 14 and follow their instructions
- If appropriate, use the 'Pan-Pan', or even 'Mayday' call on Ch 16

Some things you probably won't need to know

- If your boat (or anything on it) is over 45 m tall, you will need to get VTS's consent to navigate between Gallion's Point and Bull's Point.
- If you need Tower Bridge to be raised, you will have to give the Bridge Master 24 hours notice.
- Red lights on the piers each side of the main arch (the bascule bridge) of Tower Bridge indicate that it is closed, opening or closing. Green lights on those piers indicate that it is open.

  In restricted visibility, in addition to the green lights, a high frequency repetitive note of 820 cycles per second will be transmitted for a period of approximately 10 seconds, followed by a silent period of the same duration. These signals will be given over the loud hailer system from the north pier of the bridge for such period as the bascule bridge is open for river traffic.

- There are additional rules which relate to conduct in restricted visibility. If you should be silly or unfortunate enough to find yourself on the Thames in such conditions, talk to VTS! They will help/advise you.

Battersea Road Bridge and Beaufort Stairs

Top tips and rules

- The normal Collision Reguations apply , but with some minor local changes, so be familiar with them before venturing on the river

- Do not take to the river as skipper if under the influence of drink or drugs

- Ensure that your vessel's name is clearly marked on her, and that you have a working anchor and sufficient anchor chain/cable on board

- At bridges and rounding bends, a power driven boat navigating against the tide must slow down and even stop to avoid the risk of collision with a vessel navigating with the tide. Vessels navigating with the tide have precedence.

- The main navigation channel (the 'authorised channel') on charts is marked by pecked lines. If you are dawdling to sight-see, do so as much as possible outside the main channel so as not to hinder other craft. In any event, conditions (depth of water, air draft and so on) permitting, and save in emergency, vessels under 13·7m in length should keep out of the authorised channel.

- Come what may, do not impede vessels over 20m in length.

- Keep to the starboard side of the channel … but do not be surprised to see other vessels on your side of the river, particularly at low tide rounding promontories. So KEEP A GOOD LOOKOUT at ALL times

- Keep VHF channel 14 open to hear what is going on at all times. 'London VTS' makes regular broadcasts, and commercial traffic will use this channel to keep VTS informed of its movements. So by listening yourself, you will be able to hear what is going on around you. Keep a listening ear to Ch 16 as well if possible.

- Do not travel two abreast unless overtaking. Never overtake an overtaking vessel … so … NEVER travel three abreast

- Ferries (recognisable by the word 'FERRY' marked each side!) should give way to vessels proceeding up- or downstream.

- Keep wash down. Irrespective of any speed limits which apply, the skipper of every vessel has a duty not to cause wash which is excessive or may cause damage or danger to other river users or craft. If you do make too much wash, it is no defence to say you were within the speed limits, if any. The rule of thumb is not to exceed 10 knots in the area covered by this book....and above Wandsworth Bridge there is a limit of 8 knots. There is an advisory limit of 12 knots between Cherry Garden Pier and Wandsworth Bridge.

- The flag signal Romeo Yankee means 'Overtake me slowly', or in other words, 'Make less Wash'. It will be flown for a reason!

- The fast 'Clippers' nip onto and off their piers very quickly. If you see one mooring ahead of you, beware that it may be off again much sooner than you think.

- Also be aware that Clippers moor stern to the tide as well as more usually, bow into tide.

- Keep an especially good look out for, and keep clear of tugs towing barges, and self-propelled ballast barges. These go upriver through central London from about 3 ½ hours before high water, and downstream on the ebb tide about 1 to 3 hours after high water.

- Tidal Sets......water tries to flow in a straight line, so as a general rule, expect the tidal set (the direction that the tide flows) to set, or push you to the outside of river bends.

- Tugs and their tows are susceptible to lateral movement caused by tidal sets....so, particularly on bends in the river, give them a wide berth, and expect the tows to slew to the outside of the bends

- (Except in an emergency) do not anchor in the fairway or within 60m of any tunnels

- Walbrook Wharf (on the north bank between Cannon Street and Southwark Bridges) is a busy waste transfer station, and tugs will be encountered thereabouts navigating with tows on the wrong side of the river ...this especially on the flood tide. Listen to Ch 14 to hear the tugmasters giving their intentions to 'London VTS' who will then repeat the details as a general navigation broadcast. [1] See part 3 for the other Waste Transfer Stations.

- When there are large vessels manoeuvring in the vicinity of HMS Belfast, or if navigating Blackfriars at night[2], call 'Thames Patrol' on Ch 14 for instructions/information

[1] This is in a very busy part of the river, hence this special note
[2] This during the extensive works being carried out there

The Thames Barrier

Special rules apply for the Barrier Control Zone (between Margaret Ness and Blackwall Point)

- Radio 'London VTS' (Ch 14) for permission to go through the barrier...if inbound, at Crayford Ness, (or when you enter the river, if you are doing so above Crayford Ness.), or if outbound, when you have cleared Tower Bridge, (or when you enter the River if you are doing so below Tower Bridge). London VTS will tell you which span to use.

- Always navigate the barrier through the span marked with green arrows (and, in restricted visibility, by high intensity white lights)

- Do not anchor within 100 metres of the barrier.

- If a sailing vessel, use power when navigating the barrier.

- Only overtake within the Barrier control zone with the permission of 'London VTS'

Bridges

Putney Bridge

- Bridge arches are numbered from the northern bank.

- Bridge arches open to navigation are marked by two orange/amber lights, side by side at the highest point of each open arch. This does not mean you can't use other arches, but always be sure you have sufficient water under you boat, and headroom above it!

- Arches closed to navigation display 3 red discs in a triangle by day, and red lights in a triangle by night.

- Arches with headroom reduced below the published figures (usually for maintenance purposes) are marked by a bale or bundle of straw suspended from the arch at the height of the restriction by day, and by a white light in place of the bale at night

- The main arches are fitted with 'special lights'. These are lit remotely by large commercial vessels or by the VTS. If you see a bright white

Tower Bridge

Victoria Rail (Grosvenor) Bridge with Chelsea Bridge in the foreground. Moorings between

isophase (4secs) light over an arch , there will be one vessel using or about to use the arch. If the bright light is flashing very quickly, there will be two or more large vessels using or about to use that arch. Whichever you see, KEEP OUT THE WAY, clear of the arch, until the light is out.

- In some strong tides, rough water and large standing waves form on the river, more usually on the downstream side of some bridges. In particular, on a strong ebb tide against an easterly wind, a standing wave of a metre or so in height forms downstream of London Bridge.

- The river around Tower Bridge is always busy. Immediately downstream of the bridge are St Katherines Dock and Pier, and Butlers Wharf, where vessels are constantly coming and going. Upstream are Tower Pier, where sightseeing cruises and Thames Clippers berth, and HMS Belfast, where you may see a cruise liner manoeuvring. Take VERY special care here.

- The two Blackfriars bridges, and the remains of the old bridge, are close together, causing strong currents and eddies at some states (more on the ebb) of the tide, especially on the south (downstream) side.

Battersea Rail Bridge

By day or night 2 orange lights side by side		Navigation arch (you can go through this arch)
By day 3 red discs arranged in an upside-down triangle By night 3 red lights arranged in an upside-down triangle		Arch CLOSED to navigation
By day A bundle of straw By night 1 white light		Headroom of arch reduced (but arch still open to traffic)
By day or night A flashing white light isophase (equal periods of on and off) A very quick flashing light		A large vessel in the vicinity Two or more large vessels are in the vicinity In both cases KEEP CLEAR of the arch with the flashing light

2 Places: landmarks

Reference landmarks				Distances taken from
Barking Creek Barrier	0°05'·8 E	N Bank		The mouth of Barking Creek
The Thames Barrier	0°02'·3 E			The Thames Barrier
Millenium Dome	0°00'·2 E	S Bank		A line due N from The Dome
Royal Naval College Greenwich	0°00'·4 W	S Bank		Greenwich Pier
Tower Bridge	0°04'·5 W			Tower Bridge
The London Eye	0°07'·2 W	S Bank		London Eye
Battersea Power Station	0°08'·7 W	S Bank		Battersea Power Station
Belvedere Tower, Chelsea Harbour	0°10'·8 W	N Bank		Chelsea Harbour Pier
Putney Bridge	0°12'·8 W			Putney Bridge

Places: reaches of the Thames

Name of reach	from	to
Gallions Reach	Margaret Ness	Woolwich Arsenal
Woolwich Reach	Woolwich Arsenal	Hook Ness
Bugsby's Reach	Hook Ness	Blackwall Point
Blackwall Reach	Blackwall Point	Saunders Ness
Greenwich Reach	Saunders Ness	Masthouse Terrace Pier/Convoys Wharf
Limehouse Reach	Masthouse Terrace Pier / Convoys Wharf	Cuckolds Point/Limehouse Marina
Lower Pool	Cuckolds Point / Limehouse Marina	Cherry Garden Pier / Wapping Ness (Police Pier)
Upper Pool	Cherry Garden Pier / Wapping Ness	London Bridge
King's Reach*	London Bridge	Westminster Bridge
Lambeth Reach*	Westminster Bridge	Vauxhall Bridge
Nine Elms Reach	Vauxhall Bridge	Chelsea Bridge
Chelsea Reach	Chelsea Bridge	Battersea Bridge
Battersea Reach	Battersea Bridge	Wandsworth Bridge
Wandsworth Reach	Wandsworth Bridge	Putney Bridge
Barn Elms	Putney Bridge	upstream

* The river between Charing Cross and Westminster Bridges is included in King's Reach, although historically, there is doubt as to whether it is part of Kings, Lambeth, or indeed, none!

Places: the list

1 Name of place
2 N or S bank, or, in the case of buoys / tiers / moorings, the N or S side of the river
3 Upstream from well-known landmark
4 Downstream from well known landmark
5 The longitude in minutes, and 1/10th of a minute, E or W for each entry. For all entries, the longitude is 0°
6 The Reach of the River
7 The approximate distance of the place from London Bridge.
Positive value are for places downstream of London Bridge: negative are upstream.
Using this data, one can quickly calculate the distance between two points, and so estimate journey-times: eg From Delta Wharf (5·3) to Chelsea Harbour Pier (−4·7) is 10 nautical miles

1	2	3	4	5	6	7
NAME	N or S	UPSTREAM FROM	DOWNSTREAM FROM	0° E or W	REACH	FROM LONDON BRIDGE
Ahoy Boating Centre	S	5 cables from Greenwich	3 nm from Tower Bridge	1·4' W	Limehouse	3·5 nm
Albert Bridge	B	8 cables from Battersea Power Station	8 cables from Chelsea Harbour	10·0' W	Chelsea	−3·9 nm
Albert Wharf	S	1 nm from Battersea Power Station	6 cables from Chelsea Hrbr	10·1' W	Chelsea	−4·1 nm
Albion Riverside	S	1·1 nm from Battersea Power Station	5 cables from Chelsea Harbour	10·2' W	Chelsea	−4·2 nm
Albion Wharf	S	opposite Chelsea Harbour		10·7' W	Battersea	−4·8 nm
Alexandra Wharf	N	1·1 nm from Thames Barrier	4 cables from Dome	0·8' E	Bugsby's	6·1 nm
Angerstein Wharf	S	6 cables from Thames Barrier	9 cables from Dome	1·3' E	Woolwich	6·6 nm

Pier	Bank	Location	Location	Coord	Area	Distance
Atlas Barge Roads	S	7 cables from Thames Barrier	8 cables from Dome	1·0' E	Bugsby's	6·5 nm
Bankside Buoy	S	9 cables from Tower Bridge	1 nm from Eye	6·0' W	Kings	−0·4 nm
Bankside Pier **	S	8 cables from Tower Bridge	1·1 nm from Eye	5·8' W	Kings	−0·3 nm
Bargehouse Slip	N	1·5 nm from Barking Creek	1·2 From Thames Barrier	0·4' E	Woolwich	8·4 nm
Barking Creek Tidal Barrier	N		2·7 nm from Barrier	5·8' E	Barking / Gallions	9·9 nm
Barrier Gdn Pier	S	2·5 nm from Barking Creek	2 cables from Thames Barrier	2·5' E	Woolwich	7·4 nm
Barrier Point Pier	N	2 cables from Thames Barrier	1·3 nm from Dome	1·9' E	Woolwich	7·0 nm
Battersea (Road) Bridge	B	1 nm from Battersea Power Station	6 cables from Chelsea harbour	10·3' W	Chelsea / Battersea	−4·1 nm
Battersea Church Drawdock / Slip	S	1·4 nm from Battersea Power Station	2 cables from Chelsea harbour	10·6' W	Battersea	−4·5 nm
Battersea Church Roads	S	1·3 nm from Battersea Power Station	3 cables from Chelsea Harbour	10·6' W	Battersea	−4·4 nm
Battersea Driftwood	S	1·2 nm from Battersea Power Station	4 cables from Chelsea Harbour	10·5' W	Battersea	−4·3 nm
Battersea Mills	S	1·3 nm from Battersea Power Station	3 cables from Chelsea Harbour	10·5' W	Battersea	−4·4 nm

** Indicates piers used by Thames Clippers

Battersea Power Station	S	1·7 nm from Eye	1·6 nm from Chelsea Harbour	8·6' W	Nine Elms	−3·1 nm
Battersea Rail Bridge	B	1 cable from Chelsea Harbour	1·5 nm from Putney Bridge	10·8' W	Battersea	−4·8 nm
Battersea Wharf	S	1·1 nm from Battersea Power Station	5 cables from Chelsea Harbour	10·3' W	Battersea	−4·2 nm
Battersea Wharf 1	S	1 cable from Battersea Power Station	1.5 nm from Chelsea Harbour	8·8' W	Nine Elms	−3·2 nm
Battle Bridge Buoy	S	3 cables from Tower Bridge	1·6 nm from Eye	0·5' W	Upper Pool	0·2 nm
Bay Wharf	S	8 cables from Dome	8 cables from Greenwich	0·1' E	Blackwall	4·9 nm
Beaufort Stairs	N	1·1 nm from Battersea Power Station	5 cables from Chelsea Harbour	10·4' W	Battersea	−4·2 nm
Beckton Piers 1 & 2	N	5 & 6 cables from Barking Barrier	2·1–2·2 nm from Thames Barrier	5·0' E	Gallions	9·4 nm
Bell Lane Creek	S	9 cables from Chelsea Harbour	7 cables from Putney Bridge	11·7' W	Wandsworth	−5·6 nm
Bell Watergate Stairs	S	1·6 nm from Barking Barrier	9 cables from Thames Barrier	3·9' E	Woolwich	8·1 nm
Belmont Wharf	S	3 cables from Chelsea Harbour	1·3 nm from Putney Bridge	10·8' W	Battersea	−5·0 nm
Bethells Wharf	S	6 cables from Dome	1 nm from Greenwich	0·1' W	Blackwall	5·1 nm
Blackfriars Bridge	B	1·1 nm from Tower Bridge	8 cables from Eye	6·3' W	Kings	−0·6 nm

Name	N/S/B	Location		W/E	Reference	Distance
Blackfriars Pier **	N	1·2 nm from Tower Bridge	7 cables from Eye	6·4' W	Kings	−0·7 nm
Blackfriars Railway Bridge	B	1·1 nm from Tower Bridge	8 cables from Eye	6·2' W	Kings	−0·6 nm
Blackwall Entrance/Pierhead (West India Dock)	N	4 cables from Dome	1·2 nm from Greenwich	0·4' W	Blackwall	5·3 nm
Blackwall Point	S	at Dome	1·6 nm from Greenwich	0·2' E	Bugsby's / Blackwall	5·7 nm
Blackwall Pt Drawdock	S	4 cables from Dome	1·2 nm from Greenwich	0·1' W	Blackwall	5·3 nm
Blackwall Stairs	N	3 cables from Dome	1·3 nm from Greenwich	0·3' W	Blackwall	5·4 nm
Blyth Wharf	N	1·8 from Greenwich	1·7 nm from Tower Bridge	2·1' W	Limehouse	2·2 nm
Bow Creek	N	1·3 nm from Thames Barrier	2 cables from Dome	0·6' E	Bugsby's	5·9 nm
Brewery Wharf	S	in Deptford Creek			Greenwich	3·7 nm
Britton's Collar Moorings	N	3 cables from Tower Bridge	1·6 nm from Eye	5·0' W	Upper Pool	0·2 nm
Broomhouse Drawdock	N	1 nm from Chelsea Harbour	6 cables from Putney Bridge	11·8' W	Wandsworth	−5·7 nm
Brunswick Wharf	S	1·1 nm from Eye	6 cables from Battersea Power Station	7·6' W	Nine Elms	−2·5 nm

** indicates piers used by Thames Clippers

Pier	Side					Location	
Bull's Point (aka Gallions Point)	N	1·1 nm from Barking Barrier	1·4 nm from Barrier	4·4' E	Gallions	8·6 nm
Butlers Wharf Pier	S	3·4 nm from Greenwich	1 cable from Tower Bridge	4·4' W	Upper Pool	0·6 nm
Cadogan Pier	N	8 cables from Battersea Power Station	8 cables from Chelsea Harbour	10·0' W	Chelsea	–3·9 nm
Canary Wharf Pier**	N	1·6 nm from Greenwich	1·9 nm from Tower Bridge	1·7' W	Limehouse	2·4 nm
Cannon St Rly Bridge	B	7 cables from Tower Bridge	1·2 nm from Eye	5·5' W	Kings	–0·2 nm
Chalkstone Barge Rds Driftwood	N	1·2 nm from Greenwich	2·3 nm from Tower Bridge	1·7' W	Limehouse	2·8 nm
Chalkstone Roads	N	1·1 nm from Greenwich	2·4 nm from Tower Bridge	1·7' W	Limehouse	2·9 nm
Chambers Wharf	S	3·1 nm from Greenwich	4 cables from Tower Bridge	4·0' W	Upper Pool	0·9 nm
Charlton Pier	S	Immediately from Thames Barrier	1·5 nm from Dome	2·1' E	Woolwich	7·2 nm
Chelsea Bridge	B	2 cables from Battersea Power Station	1·4 nm from Chelsea harbour	9·0' W	Nine Elms / Chelsea	–3·3 nm
Chelsea Driftwood	S	4 cables from Battersea Power Station	1·2 nm from Chelsea Harbour	9·3' W	Chelsea	–3·5 nm
Chelsea Harbour Pier	N	1·6 nm from Battersea Power Station	1·6 nm from Putney Bridge	10·8' W	Chelsea	–4·7 nm
Chelsea Wharf	N	1·3 from Battersea Power Station	3 cables from Chelsea Harbour	10·7' W	Battersea	–4·4 nm

** Indicates piers used by Thames Clippers

Name	N/S					
Chelsea Yacht and Boat Co	N	1·2 nm from Battersea Power Station	4 cables from Chelsea Harbour	10·7' W	Battersea	−4·3 nm
Cherry Garden Pier	S	3 nm from Greenwich	5 cables from Tower Bridge	3·7' W	Lower / Upper Pool	1·0 nm
China Wharf	S	3·3 mn from Greenwich	2 cables from Tower Bridge	4·2' W	Upper Pool	0·7 nm
City Cruises Moorings	S	2·8 nm from Greenwich	7 cables from Tower Bridge	3·6' W	Upper Pool	1·2 nm
Civil & Marine	S	4 cables from Dome	1·2 nm from Greenwich	0·1' W	Blackwall	5·3 nm
Clarence Wharf	S	2·5 nm from Greenwich	1 nm from Tower Bridge	2·9' W	Lower Pool	1·5 nm
Coin St Moorings	S	1·3 nm from Tower Bridge	6 cables from Eye	6·6' W	Kings	−0·8 nm
Comleys Wharf (RMC Fulham)	N	6 cables from Chelsea Harbour	1 nm from Putney Bridge	11·2' W	Battersea	−5·3 nm
Convoys Wharf	S	7 cables from Greenwich	2·8 nm from Tower Bridge	1·7' W	Limehouse	3·3 nm
Cory's Pier / Yard	S	4 cables from Thames Barrier	1·1 nm from Dome	1·6' E	Woolwich	6·8 nm
Cremorne Wharf	N	1·3 nm from Battersea Power Station	3 cables from Chelsea Harbour	10·8' W	Battersea	−4·4 nm
Cricketers Stairs	N	1·0 nm from Battersea Power Station	6 cables from Chelsea Harbour	10·2' W	Chelsea	−4·1 nm

Location	N/S	Distance	Distance	Bearing	Reach	
Cringle Dock / Wharf	S	1·6 nm from Eye	1 cable from Battersea Power Station	8·5' W	Nine Elms	−3·0 nm
Crysanthemum Pier	N	1·3 nm from Tower Bridge	6 cables from Eye	6·6' W	Kings	−0·8 nm
Cuckold's Point	S	2·8 nm from Greenwich	1·7 nm from Tower Bridge	2·1' W	Limehouse	2·2 nm
Cyclops Wharf	N	8 cables from Greenwich	2·7 nm from Tower Bridge	1·5' W	Limehouse	3·2 nm
DePass Wharf	N	at Barking Creek				9·9 nm
Deanston Wharf	N	5 cables from Thames Barrier	1 nm from Dome	1·4' E	Woolwich	6·7 nm
Debden Wharf	N	at Barking Creek				9·9 nm
Delta Wharf	S	4 cables from Dome	1·2 nm from Greenwich	0·1' W	Blackwall	5·3 nm
Deptford Creek	S	3 cables from Greenwich	3·2 nm from Tower Bridge	1·1' W	Greenwich	3·7 nm
Deptford Powergen Wharf	S	4 cables from Greenwich	3·1 nm from Tower Bridge	1·3' W	Greenwich	3·6 nm
Dock Entrance Wharf	N	1·1 nm from Thames Barrier	4 cables from Dome	0·8' E	Bugsby's	6·1 nm
Docklands Wharf	N	at Barking Creek				9·9 nm

Dohm Wharf	N	1·1 nm from Thames Barrier	4 Cables from Dome	0·9' E	Bugsby's	6·1 nm
Duggens	N	1·2 nm from Thames Barrier	3 cables from Dome	0·7' E	Bugsby's	6·0 nm
Duresco Wharf	S	2 cables from Thames Barrier	1·3 nm from Dome	1·9' E	Woolwich	7·0 nm
Durham Wharf	S	4 cables from Thames Barrier	1·1 nm from Dome	1·7' E	Woolwich	6·8 nm
East India Dock	N	1·5 nm from Thames Barrier	due N of Dome	0·2' E	Bugsby's / Blackwall	5·7 nm
East Woolwich Tiers / Moorings	S	1·4 nm from Barking Creek	1·3 nm from Thames Barrier	4·4' E	Woolwich	8·5 nm
Elm Quay	S	1·3 nm from Eye	4 cables from Battersea Power Station	8·0' W	Nine Elms	–2·7 nm
Embankment Pier **	N	1·7 nm from Tower Bridge	2 cables from Eye	7·3' W	Kings	–1·2 nm
Essex Buoy / Mill Stairs	S	3·1 nm from Greenwich	4 cables from Tower Bridge	3·9' W	Upper Pool	0·9 nm
Falcon Wharf	S	2 cables from Chelsea Harbour	1·4 nm from Putney Bridge	10·7' W	Battersea	–4·9 nm
Feathers Wharf	S	9 cables from Chelsea Harbour	7 cables from Putney Bridge	11·7' W	Wandsworth	–5·6 nm
Festival Pier	S	1·5 nm from Tower Bridge	2 cables from Eye	7·1' W	Kings	–1·0 nm
Foley Buoy	N	1·5 nm from Barking Creek	1·2 nm from Thames Barrier	4·1' E	Woolwich	8·4 nm

** Indicates piers used by Thames Clippers

Folly House Barge Roads	N	7 cables from Dome	0·3' W	9 cables from Greenwich	Blackwall	5·0 nm
Free Trade Wharf	N	2·2 nm from Greenwich	2·7' W	1·3 nm from Tower Bridge	Lower Pool/Limehouse	1·8 nm
Fulham Railway Bridge	B	1·4 nm from Chelsea Harbour	12·6' W	2 cables from Putney Bridge	Wandsworth	−6·1 nm
Fulham Wharf	N	5 cables from Chelsea Harbour	11·2' W	1·1 nm from Putney Bridge	Battersea	−5·2 nm
Gallions Barge Roads	S	6 cables from Barking Creek	5·2' E	2·1 nm from Thames Barrier	Gallions	9·3 nm
Gallions Point (aka Bull's Point)	N	1·1 nm from Barking Barrier	4·4' E	1·4 nm from Thames Barrier	Gallions	8·6 nm
Gallions Point marina	N	9 cables from Barking Barrier	9·0' E	1·8 nm from Thames Barrier	Gallions	8·7 nm
Gallions Reach Driftwood	S	9 cables from Barking Creek	5·1' E	1·8 nm from Thames Barrier	Gallions	9·0 nm
Gargoyle Wharf	S	6 cables from Chelsea Harbour	11·1' W	1 nm from Putney Bridge	Battersea	−5·3 nm
Georges Stairs	S	3·3 nm from Greenwich	4·3' W	2 cables from Tower Bridge	Upper Pool	0·7 nm
Granite Wharf	S	1·2 nm from Dome	0·1' E	4 cables from Greenwich	Blackwall / Greenwich	4·5 nm
Great Eastern Pier/Masthouse Terrace	N	6 cables from Greenwich	1·3' W	2·9nm from Tower Bridge	Greenwich / Limehouse	3·4 nm

Name	Side					Distance
Greenland Pier **	S	1·2 nm from Greenwich	2·3 nm from Tower Bridge	1·9' W	Limehouse	2·8 nm
Greenwich Driftwood	S	1·5 nm from Dome	1 cables from Greenwich	0·4' W	Greenwich	4·2 nm
Greenwich Pier **	S	1·6nm from Dome	3·5 nm from Tower Bridge	0·6' W	Greenwich	4·0 nm
Greenwich Power Station	S	1·3 nm from Dome	3 cables from Greenwich	0·1' W	Greenwich	4·4 nm
Greenwich Ship Tiers	S	2 cables from Greenwich	3·3 from Tower Bridge	0·9' W	Greenwich	3·8 nm
Greenwich Y C	S	6 cables from Thames Barrier	9 cables from Dome	1·1' E	Woolwich	6·6 nm
Grosvenor Bridge (Victoria Railwayy Bridge)	B	1 cable from Battersea Power Station	1·5 nm from Chelsea Harbour	8·9' W	Nine Elms	–3·2 nm
Grosvenor College Stairs	N	4 cables from Battersea Power Station	1·2 nm from Chelsea Harbour	9·3' W	Chelsea	–3·5 nm
Grosvenor Dock	N	2 cables from Battersea Power Station	1·4 nm from Chelsea Harbour	9·0' W	Nine Elms	–3·3 nm
Grosvenor Pier	N	1·3 nm from Eye	4 cables from Battersea Power Station	8·1' W	Nine Elms	–2·7 nm
Gulf (Island) Jetty	N	4 cables from Thames Barrier	1·1 nm from Dome	1·5' E	Woolwich	6·8 nm
HMS Belfast	S	2 cables from Tower Bridge	1·7 nm from Eye	4·9' W	Upper Pool	0·3 nm

** Indicates piers used by Thames Clippers

HMS President	N	1·3 nm from Tower Bridge	6 cables from Eye	6·5' W	Kings	–0·8 nm
HQS Wellington	N	1·4 nm from Tower Bridge	5 cables from Eye	6·7' W	Kings	–0·9 nm
Hanover Hole	See note	2·5 nm from Greenwich	1 nm from Tower Bridge	2·8' W	Lower Pool	1·5 nm
Heiko (Fuel barge Heiko)	N	3·3 nm from Greenwich	2 cables from Tower Bridge	4·1' W	Upper Pool	0·7 nm
Hermitage Stairs Moorings	N	3·2 nm from Greenwich	3 cables from Tower Bridge	4·0' W	Upper Pool	0·8 nm
Hermitage Wharf / Moorings	N	3·2 nm from Greenwich	3 cables from Tower Bridge	4·0' W	Upper Pool	0·8 nm
Hispaniola	N	1·7 nm from Tower Bridge	2 cables from Eye	7·3' W	Kings	–1·2 nm
Hook Ness	N	6 cables from Barrier	8 cables from Dome	1·2' E	Bugsby's / Woolwich	6·5 nm
Hop Pole Roads	S	2·7 nm from Greenwich	8 cables from Tower Bridge	3·3' W	Lower Pool	1·3 nm
Houses of Parliament	N	3 cables from Eye	1·4 nm from Battersea Power Station	7·4' W	Lambeth	–1·7 nm
Hungerford (Charing X) Railway Bridge	B	1·7 nm from Tower Bridge	2 cables from Eye	7·2' W	Kings	–1·2 nm

Note Hanover Hole is an area of the river north of the entrance to the old Surrey Dock. Beware of large ships swinging here, in preparation for navigating under Tower Bridge

Hurlingham Y C	N	1 nm from Chelsea Harbour	6 cables from Putney Bridge	11·9' W	Wandsworth	–5·7 nm
Hurlingham Y C lift out facility (Fulham R B)	S	1·4 nm from Chesea Harbour	1 cable from Putney Bridge	12·6' W	Wandsworth	–6·1 nm
Imperial Wharf	N	1 cable from Chelsea Harbour	1·5 nm from Putney Bridge	10·9' W	Battersea	–4·8 nm
Iron Pier	S	1·1 nm from Barking Barrier	1·6 nm from Thames Barrier	4·7' E	Gallions / Woolwich	8·8 nm
Island Jetty	N	4 cables from Thames Barrier	1·1 nm from Dome	1·5' E	Woolwich	6·8 nm
Johnson Drawdock	N	opposite Greenwich Pier		0·6' W	Greenwich	4·0 nm
Kierbeck & Steel Wharves	N	at Barking Creek				9·9 nm
King George V Dock	N	1 nm from Barking barrier	1·7 nm from Thames Barrier	4·5' E	Gallions	8·9 nm
Lacks Dock	S	1 nm from Eye	7 cables from Battersea Power Station	7·4' W	Lambeth	–2·4 nm
Lambeth Bridge	B	5 cables from Eye	1·2 nm from Battersea Power Station	7·3' W	Lambeth	–1·9 nm
Lambeth Pier	S	5 cables from Eye	1·2 nm from Battersea Power Station	7·3' W	Lambeth	–1·9 nm
Lambeth River Station (LFB Fire Float)	S	6 cables from Eye	1·1 nm from Battersea Power Station	7·3' W	Lambeth	–2·0 nm

Lifeboat Pier	N	1·6 nm from Tower Bridge	3 cables from Eye	7·0' W	Kings	–1·1 nm
Limehouse Marina/Basin	N	2nm from Greenwich	1·5nm from Tower Bridge	2·2' W	Limehouse / Lower Pool	2·0 nm
Limekiln Dock entrance	N	1·8 nm from Greenwich	1·7 nm from Tower Bridge	1·9' W	Limehouse	2·2 nm
Livetts Moorings	S	3·4 nm from Greenwich	1 cable from Tower Bridge	4·4' W	Upper Pool	0·6 nm
London Bridge	B	4·5 cables from Tower Bridge	1·5 nm from Eye	5·3' W	Upper Pool / Kings	0·0 nm
London Bridge City Pier	S	4 cables from Tower Bridge	1·5 nm from Eye	5·1' W	Upper Pool	0·1 nm
London Eye Pier **	S	1·9 nm from Tower Bridge	1·7 nm from Battersea P Stn	7·2' W	Kings	–1·4 nm
London Yard (Yacht Moorings)	N	8 cables from Dome	8 cables from Greenwich	0·3' W	Blackwall	4·9 nm
Lovell's	S	1·2 nm from Dome	4 cables from Greenwich	0·0'	Greenwich	4·5 nm
Lower Gun Wharf	N	2·7 nm from Greenwich	8 cables from Tower Bridge	3·3' W	Lower Pool	1·3 nm
Lower Gun Wharf Driftwood	N	2·7 nm from Greenwich	8 cables from Tower Bridge	3·3' W	Lower Pool	1·3 nm
MI6 Building	S	9 cables from Eye	8 cables from Battersea Power Station	7·5' W	Lambeth	–2·3 nm

** Indicates piers used by Thames Clippers

Manhatten Wharf	N	7 cables from Thames Barrier	8 cables from Dome	1·2' E	Bugsby's	6·5 nm
Margaret Ness	S	3 cables from Barking Barrier	2·4 nm from Thames Barrier	5·5' E	Barking / Gallions	9·6 nm
Masthouse Terrace Pier ** (Gt E: Pier)	N	6 cables from Greenwich	2·9 nm from Tower Bridge	1·3' W	Greenwich / Limehouse	3·4 nm
Mayer Parry Wharf	N	in Bow Creek		0·6' W	Bugsby's	5·9 nm
Metro Greenham	S	1·6 from Eye	1 cable from Battersea Power Station	8·5' W	Nine Elms	–3·0 nm
Middle Wharf (RMC Vauxhall)	S	1·4 nm from Eye	3 cables from Battersea Power Station	8·1' W	Nine Elms	–2·8 nm
Mill Stairs/Essex Bouy	S	3·1 nm from Greenwich	4 cables from Tower Bridge	3·9' W	Upper Pool	0·9 nm
Millbank Millennium Pier **	N	7 cables from Eye	1 nm from Battersea Power Station	7·5' W	Lambeth	–2·1 nm
Millennium Footbridge	B	9 cables from Tower Bridge	1 nm from Eye	5·9' W	Kings	–0·4 nm
Millwall Driftwood	N	9 cables from Dome	7 cables from Greenwich	0·2' W	Blackwall	4·8 nm
Millwall Slip	N	1 cable from Greenwich	3·4 nm from Tower Bridge	0·8' W	Greenwich	3·9 nm
Millwall Wharf	N	9 cables from Dome	7 cables from Greenwich	0·2'W	Blackwall	4·8 nm

** Indicates Piers used by Thames Clippers.

Minoco Wharf	N	2 cables from Thames Barrier	1·3 nm from Dome	1·8' E	Woolwich	7·0 nm
Mohawk Wharf	N	6 cables from Thames Barrier	9 cables from Dome	1·3' E	Woolwich	6·6 nm
Murphy's Wharf	S	5 cables from Thames Barrier	1 nm from Dome	1·4' E	Woolwich	6·7 nm
Nelson (also Hilton) Pier	S	1·6 nm from Greenwich	1·9 nm from Tower Bridge	1·9' W	Limehouse	2·4 nm
Newcastle Draw Dock	N	1·3 nm from Dome	3 cables from Greenwich	0·3' W	Greenwich	4·4 nm
Nine Elms Barge Road	S	1·3 nm from Eye	4 cables from Battersea Power Station	8·0' W	Nine Elms	−2·7 nm
Nine Elms Driftwood	S	1·3 nm from Eye	6 cables from Battersea Power Station	7·7' W	Nine Elms	−2·5 nm
Nine Elms Pier	S	1·5 nm from Eye	2 cables from Battersea Power Station	8·3' W	Nine Elms	−2·9 nm
North Greenwich Pier **	S	1·2 from Thames Barrier	3 cables from Dome	0·5' E	Bugsby's	6·0 nm
North Woolwich Pier	N	1·7 nm from Barking Creek	1nm from Thames Barrier	3·8' E	Woolwich	8·2 nm
Northumberland Wharf	N	4 cables from Dome	1·2 nm from Greenwich	0·4' W	Blackwall	5·3 nm
Old Bargehouse Stairs	S	1·3 nm from Tower Bridge	6 cables from Eye	6·5' W	Kings	−0·8 nm
Old Ferry Wharf (Chelsea Yt & Bt Co)	N	1·3 nm from Battersea P Stn	3 cables from Chelsea Harbour	10·7' W	Battersea	−4·4 nm

** Indicates piers used by Thames Clippers

Name	N/S	Reference 1	Reference 2			nm
Old Victoria Dock	N	1·1 nm from Thames Barrier	4 cables from Dome	0·8' E	Bugsby's	6·1 nm
Oliver Wharf	N	3 nm from Greenwich	5 cables from Tower Bridge	3·7' W	Lower Pool	1·0 nm
Orchard Wharf	N	1·5 nm from Thames Barrier	opposite Dome	0·3' E	Bugsby's	5·7 nm
Ordnance Wharf	S	2 cables from Dome	1·4 nm from Greenwich	0·1' W	Blackwall	5·5 nm
Oxo Tower/Wharf	S	1·3 nm from Tower Bridge	6 cables from Eye	6·5' W	Kings	–0·8 nm
Oyster Wharf	S	1 cable from Chelsea Harbour	1·5 nm from Putney Bridge	10·7' W	Battersea	–4·8 nm
Peartree Wharf	S	6 cables from Thames Barrier	9 cables from Dome	1·1' E	Woolwich	6·6 nm
Peruvian Wharf	N	9 cables from Thames Barrier	6 cables from Dome	1·0' E	Bugsby's	6·3 nm
Pier Wharf	S	7 cables from Chelsea Harbour	9 cables from Putney Bridge	11·3' W	Wandsworth	–5·4 nm
Pinns Wharf	N	at Barking Creek				9·9 nm
Pipers Wharf	S	1·1 nm from Dome	5 cables from Greenwich	0·1' E	Blackwall	4·6 nm
Plaistow Wharf	N	8 cables from Thames Barrier	7 cables from Dome	1·1' E	Bugsby's	6·4 nm

Plantation Wharf / Jetty	S	4 cables from Chelsea Harbour	1·2 nm from Putney Bridge	10·9' W	Battersea	–5·1 nm
Point Pleasant Marina / Wharf	S	1·1 nm from Chelsea Harbour	5 cables from Putney Bridge	11·9' W	Wandsworth	–5·8 nm
Point Wharf	S	4 cables from Dome	1·2 nm from Greenwich	0·1' W	Blackwall	5·3 nm
Poplar Rowing Club	N	opposite Greenwich Pier		0·6' W	Greenwich	4·0 nm
President Quay	N	3·3 nm from Greenwich	2 cables from Tower Bridge	4·3' W	Upper Pool	0·7 nm
Princes Wharf	S	9 cables from Battersea Power Station	7 cables from Chelsea harbour	10·0' W	Chelsea	–4·0 nm
Priors Wharf	N	in Bow Creek		0·6' E	Bugsbys	5·9 nm
Prospect Quay	S	1·1 nm from Chelsea Harbour	5 cables from Putney Bridge	12·0' W	Wandsworth	–5·8 nm
Prospect Wharf	N	2·4 from Greenwich	1·1 nm from Tower Bridge	3·0' W	Lower Pool	1·6 nm
Putney Bridge	B	1·6 from Chelsea harbour	Chiswick / Barnes	12·7' W	Wandsworth / Barn Elms	–6·3 nm
Putney Pier	S	1 cable from Putney Bridge		13·0' W	Barn Elms	–6·4 nm
Putney Wharf	S	1·6 from Chelsea harbour	immediately from Putney Bridge	12·8' W	Wandsworth	–6·3 nm
Queen Elizabeth II Pier (N Greenwich Pier)	S	1·1 nm from Thames Barrier	4 cables from Dome	0·5' E	Bugsby's	6·1 nm

Name	N/S					
RMC Fulham (Comleys Wharf)	N	6 cables from Chelsea Harbour	1 nm from Putney Bridge	11·2' W	Battersea	−5·3 nm
RMC Vauxhall (Middle Wharf)	S	1·4 nm from Eye	3 cables from Battersea Power Station	8·1' W	Nine Elms	−2·8 nm
Ransomes Dock	S	9 cables from Battersea Power Station	7 cables from Chelsea Harbour	10·1' W	Chelsea	−4·0 nm
Reeds Wharf	S	3·3 nm from Greenwich	2 cables from Tower Bridge	4·2' W	Upper Pool	0·7 nm
Reuters Pier **	N	2 cables from Dome	1·4 nm from Greenwich	0·2' W	Blackwall	5·5 nm
Rippleway Wharf	N	at Barking Creek				9·9 nm
Riverside Wharf	S	1 cable from Thames Barrier	1·4 nm from Dome	2·0' E	Woolwich	7·1 nm
Royal Albert Dock	N	8 cables from Barking Creek	1·9 nm from Thames Barrier	4·7' E	Gallions	9·1 nm
Royal Arsenal Pier **	S	1·5 nm from Barking Creek	1·2 nm Thames Barrier	4·3' E	Gallions / Woolwich	8·4 nm
Sacrificial Buoy (Starvation Moorings)	N	1·6 nm from Barking Creek	1·1 nm from Thames Barrier	4·0' E	Woolwich	8·3 nm
Sainsbury's Jetty	N	4 cables from Chelsea Harbour	1·2 nm from Putney Bridge	11·1' W	Battersea	−5·1 nm
Savoy Pier	N	1·6 nm from Tower Bridge	3 cables from Eye	7·2' W	Kings	−1·1 nm
South Dock Marina	S	1·1 nm from Greenwich	2·4 nm from Tower Bridge	2·0' W	Limehouse	2·9 nm

** Indicates piers used by Thames Clippers

Southwark Bridge	B	7 cables from Tower Bridge	1·2 nm from Eye	5·6' W	Kings	−0·2 nm
St Botolph's moorings	N	3 cables from Tower Bridge	1·6 nm from Eye	5·0' W	Upper Pool	0·2 nm
St Georges Wharf / Pier **	S	1 nm from Eye	7 cables from Battersea Power Station	7·6' W	Nine Elms	−2·4 nm
St Katherine's Dock / Haven / Pier	N	3·4nm from Greenwich	1 cable from Tower Bridge	4·4' W	Upper Pool	0·6 nm
St Mary Overy Dock	S	6 cables from Tower Bridge	1·3 nm from Eye	5·4' W	Kings	0·1 nm
St Saviours Dock	S	3·3 nm from Greenwich	2 cables from Tower Bridge	4·3' W	Upper Pool	0·7 nm
St Thomas's Passenger Boat Moorings	S	3 cables from Eye	1·4 nm from Battersea Power Station	7·3' W	Lambeth	−1·7 nm
Starvation Moorings (Sacrificial Buoy)	N	1·6 nm from Barking Creek	1·1 nm from Thames barrier	4·0' E	Woolwich	8·3 nm
Stone Stairs Roads / Tier	N	2·2 nm from Greenwich	1·3 nm from Tower Bridge	2·7' W	Lower Pool	1·8 nm
Surrey Basin / Commercial Dock	S	2·4 nm from Greenwich	1·1 nm from Tower Bridge	2·9' W	Lower Pool	1·6 nm
Swan Lane Pier	N	5 cables from Tower Bridge	1·4 nm from Eye	5·3' W	Kings	0·0 nm
Swedish Wharf	N	6 cables from Chelsea Harbour	1 nm from Putney Bridge	11·3' W	Battersea	−5·3 nm

** Indicates piers used by Thames Clippers

T Jetty	S	1·2 nm from Barking Creek	1·5 nm from Thames Barrier	4·6' E	Gallions	8·7 nm
Tamesis Dock	S	8 cables from Eye	9 cables from Battersea Power Station	7·4' W	Lambeth	–2·2 nm
Tate & Lyles Jetty	N	2·3 nm from Barking Creek	4 cables from Thames Barrier	2·8' E	Woolwich	7·6 nm
Tattershall Castle	N	1·8 nm from Tower Bridge	1 cable from Eye	7·3' W	Kings	–1·3 nm
Temple Driftwood	N	1·5 nm from Tower Bridge	4 cables from Eye	6·8' W	Kings	–1·0 nm
Temple Pier	N	1·5 nm from Tower Bridge	4 cables from Eye	6·9' W	Kings	–1·0 nm
Thames Barrier YC Pier	S	8 cables from Thames Barrier	7 cables from Dome	0·9' E	Bugsby's	6·4 nm
Thames Court (Bull Wharf)	N	8 cables from Tower Bridge	1·1 nm from Eye	5·7' W	Kings	–0·3 nm
Thames House Pierhead	N	9 cables from Barking Creek	1·8 nm from Thames Barrier	4·7' E	Gallions	9·0 nm
Thames Refinery	N	2·3 nm from Barking Creek	4 cables from Thames Barrier	2·9' E	Woolwich	7·6 nm
Thames Refueller	S	4 cables from Eye	1·3 nm from Battersea Power Station	7·3' W	Lambeth	–1·8 nm

Location						nm
Thames Tunnel Mills/ Church Stairs	S	2·7 nm from Greenwich	8 cables from Tower Bridge	3·2' W	Lower Pool	1·3 nm
Thames Wharf (Bow)	N	1·2nm from Thames Barrier	3 cables from Dome	0·7' E	Bugsby's	6·0 nm
Thames Wharf (Charlton/Woolwich)	S	1 cable from Thames Barrier	1·4 nm from Dome	2·1' E	Woolwich	7·1 nm
Tower Bridge	B	3·5 nm from Greenwich	1·9 nm from Eye	4·5' W	Lower/ Upper Pool	0·5 nm
Tower Bridge yacht mooring	S	< 1 cable from Tower Bridge		4·6' W	Upper Pool	0·5 nm
Tower Driftwood	S	3·2 nm from Greenwich	3 cables from Tower Bridge	4·1' W	Upper Pool	0·8 nm
Tower Pier **	N	2 cables from Tower Bridge	1·7 nm from Eye	4·7' W	Upper Pool	0·3 nm
Tower Stairs	N	2 cables from Tower Bridge	1·7 nm from Eye	4·8' W	Upper Pool	0·2 nm
Trinity Buoy Wharf	N	1·4 nm from Thames Barrier	1 cable from Dome	0·4' E	Bugsby's	5·8 nm
Trinity Jubilee Pier **	N	1·4 nm from Thames Barrier	1 cable from Dome	0·4' E	Bugsby's	5·8 nm
Tunnel Glucose	S	1 nm from Dome	6 cables from Greenwich	0·1' E	Blackwall	4·7 nm
Tunnel Pier	N	2·8 nm from Greenwich	7 cables from Tower Bridge	3·4' W	Lower Pool	1·2 nm

** Indicates piers used by Thames Clippers

Location	Type	Distance 1	Distance 2	Bearing	Area	nm
Union Wharf Moorings	N	1·6 nm from Greenwich	1·9 nm from Tower Bridge	1·7' W	Limehouse	2·4 nm
Vauxhall Bridge	B	1 nm from Eye	7 cables from Battersea P Stn	7·6' W	Lambeth/Nine Elms	−2·4 nm
Victoria Emb: RNLI Station	N	1·6 nm from Tower Bridge	3 cables from Eye	7·0' W	Kings	−1·1 nm
Victoria Rly Bridge (Grosvenor Bridge)	B	1 cable from Battersea P Stn	1·5 nm from Chelsea Harbour	8·9' W	Nine Elms	−3·2 nm
Victoria Stone Wharf	N	at Barking Creek				9·9 nm
Victoria deep water terminal	S	7 cables from Dome	9 cables from Greenwich	0·1' W	Blackwall	5·0 nm
Vintry House Stairs	N	8 cables from Tower Bridge	1·1 nm from Eye	5·7' W	Kings	−0·3 nm
Virgin Heliport (also Westland Heliport)	S	2 cables from Chelsea Harbour	1·4 nm from Putney Bridge	10·8' W	Battersea	−4·9 nm
Walbrook Wharf	N	7 cables from Tower Bridge	1·2 nm from Eye	5·5' W	Kings	−0·2 nm
Wandsworth Bridge	B	6 cables from Chelsea Harbour	1 nm from Putney Bridge	11·3' W	Battersea/Wandsworth	−5·3 nm
Wandsworth Driftwood	S	1·2 nm from Chelsea Harbour	4 cables from Putney Bridge	12·1' W	Wandsworth	−5·9 nm
Wapping Pier	N	2·8 nm from Greenwich	7 cables from Tower Bridge	3·4' W	Lower Pool	1·2 nm

Name	N/S					Distance
Wapping Police Pier	N	2·9 nm from Greenwich	6 cables from Tower Bridge	3·5' W	Upper Pool	1·1 nm
Ware Point	S	5 cables from Barking Creek	2·2 nm from Thames Barrier	5·3' E	Gallions	9·4 nm
Warren Lane Buoy	S	1·6 nm from Barking Creek	1·1 nm from Thames Barrier	4·3' E	Woolwich	8·3 nm
Warspite Moorings	S	2·3 nm from Barking Creek	4 cables from Thames Barrier	2·9' E	Woolwich	7·6 nm
Watergate Stairs	S	6 cables from Greenwich	2·9 nm from Tower Bridge	1·5' W	Greenwich/ Limehouse	3·4 nm
Waterloo Millenium Pier	S	at The Eye		7·2' W	Kings	−1·4 nm
Welbeck Wharf	N	at Barking Creek				9·9 nm
West India Dock	N	5 cables from Dome	1·1 nm from Greenwich	0·5' W	Blackwall	5·2 nm
West India Dock Pier (disused)	N	1·4 miles from Greenwich	2·1 nm from Tower Bridge	1·7' W	Limehouse	2·6 nm
Western Riverside Waste Transfer Stn	S	8 cables from Chelsea Harbour	8 cables from Putney Bridge	11·5' W	Wandsworth	−5·5 nm
Westland Heliport (also Virgin Heliport)	S	2 cables from Chelsea Harbour	1·4 nm from Putney Bridge	10·8' W	Battersea	−4·9 nm

Location	Side	Reference 1	Reference 2	Bearing	Area	Distance
Westminster Boating Base	N	1·3 nm from Eye	4 cables from Battersea Power Station	8·1' W	Nine Elms	–2·7 nm
Westminster Bridge	B	2 cables from Eye	1·5 nm from Battersea Power Station	7·3' W	Kings/ Lambeth	–1·6 nm
Westminster Pier	N	1 cable from Eye	1·6 nm from Battersea Power Station	7·4' W	Kings	–1·5 nm
Whitehall Stairs	N	opposite the Eye		7·4' W	Kings	–1·4 nm
William IV Stairs	N	1·6 nm from Eye	1 cable from Battersea Power Station	8·5' W	Nine Elms	–3·0 nm
Woods Buoy	S	3 cables from Thames Barrier	1·2 nm from Dome	1·7' E	Bugsby's	6·9 nm
Woolwich Arsenal	S	1·2 nm from Barking Creek	1·5 from Thames Barrier	4·6' E	Gallions/ Woolwich	8·7 nm
Woolwich Ferry	N& S	1·8 nm from Barking Creek	9 cables from Thames Barrier	3·8' E	Woolwich	8·1 nm
Woolwich Reach Driftwood	S	2·3 nm from Barking Creek	4 cables from Thames Barrier	3·0' E	Woolwich	7·6 nm
Yorkshire Grey Stairs	N	8 cables from Battersea Power Station	8 cables from Chelsea Harbour	9·9' W	Chelsea	–3·9 nm

3 The journey up the river

See fold-out plan opposite

I make no apologies for reiterating here some points made above. The River Thames is a very busy place. You are likely to encounter craft of all sizes, some of which are more sea-worthy than others! On your journey through London, you may be sharing the water with a warship, a rowing boat, a narrow-boat, a high speed rib and a tug and tow. You will almost certainly rub shoulders with a multitude of large passenger craft, and PLA and police launches. Whilst all this may seem intimidating, if you abide by the rules, and use common sense (seamanship), your experience should prove exciting and safe.

Before you start

- Learn the International Regulations for Preventing Collisions at Sea, and the local amendments to the general rules (see pages 4–8.

- Prepare a passage plan. In doing so, you will of necessity satisfy yourself that your boat and crew are up to the trip.

Your vessel should be in good order, have its name clearly marked on it, have a suitable anchor ready to use, and ideally, have a working VHF set on board. You will also note the tides, the headroom under bridges, and the shallows (shoals) to be aware of. You will also note hazards, which is where I really start this section.

Union Wharf, Trinity Jubilee Pier

Hazards

- There are very many moorings of various sorts on each side of the river: too many to be individually listed here, although I mention some as being of particular note on the fold-out plan opposite. Suffice to say that your charts will show these, and your eyes will see them! Remember, where there are mooring buoys there are likely to be vessel movements on and off them!

- The river is tidal, so do keep a close eye on the depth of water. Your charts will show charted depths, and tide tables will tell you predicted tidal heights. But don't forget that the predictions may well be wrong. It is not uncommon for tidal heights to be 0·5m below prediction! London VTS, in its regular information broadcasts will tell you if the actual tidal heights are materially different to the predicted heights.

- The Port of London Authority issues frequent Notices to Mariners, which warn of navigational hazards, both temporary, and permanent.

  Before you embark on your trip, and as part of your passage planning, you should have a look at www.pla.co.uk/notice2mariners and determine which, if any, notices are relevant to you.

- Tugs with tows are likely to be encountered anywhere, and more particularly above half-tide. Be very aware that the tidal stream and surprising sets may well cause these vessels to be on the wrong side of the river. There are several Waste Transfer Stations which are served by tugs towing barges. These are identified on the foldout plan but as a general rule, keep your eyes and ears open, and give these large, not-so-nimble hazards a wide berth.

- Narrow Canal boats use the river like everyone else, particularly upstream from Limehouse, which is one of the main points where the non-tidal, inland waterways system joins the tidal river. Be aware!

- Bridges! Ensure that you have checked that you will have sufficient clearance, both under your keel, and under the arch. Beware of currents increasing particularly close to bridge piers, and of 'shoulders' to the piers under the surface of the water. Do your homework.